plant dye
zine

PUBLISHED BY

REBECCA DESNOS

Plant Dye Zine is independently published
by Rebecca Desnos.

rebeccadesnos.com / info@rebeccadesnos.com

Instagram: @rebeccadesnos

Logo by Rebecca Desnos

ISBN 978-0-9955566-8-3 (paperback)
ISBN 978-0-9955566-1-4 (eBook)

Published by Rebecca Desnos, in 2020, in the UK.

Photos on pages 1 & 2 are by Annie Spratt. Photo on page 3 is by Rebecca Desnos

Buddleja (purple flowers) and goldenrod (yellow) make beautiful dyes and inks.

Hi! I'm Rebecca Desnos—a natural dyer in the UK, a writer, a mother to two young children, and an all-round plant lover.

I'm passionate about making colours from local plants and showing others how they can do the same!

Get in touch

Do you have any comments or questions about this Plant Dye Zine? I'd love to hear from you!

info@rebeccadesnos.com

Portrait by Siobhan Watts / Background photo by Annie Spratt

welcome!

I'm thrilled to share my latest offering with you—this Plant Dye Zine! This little book contains some of my own tutorials, and I've brought together recipes and articles from other natural dyers from around the world. I hope that one of the tutorials will tempt you enough to give it a go, and you may discover a brand new passion! Even if you're an experienced natural dyer, I think there will be some inspiring nuggets within these pages.

Learn how to bundle dye, pound plants onto fabric (it's a brand new tutorial!), start a dye garden, and make inks and paint. As a plant lover, I thought you'd enjoy the bonus flower pressing tutorial at the end!

I'd love to see you try out these projects, so please share with me on Instagram by tagging @rebeccadesnos. Happy plant dyeing!

Rebecca x

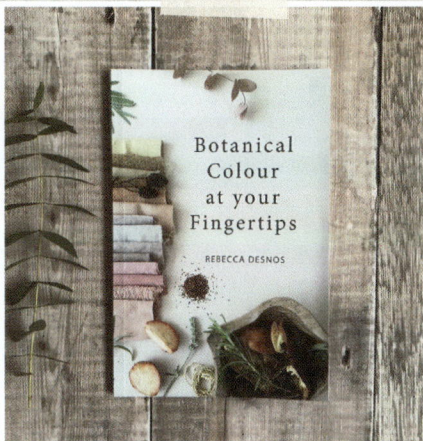

Botanical Dyeing

Learn more of my dye methods in my book, *Botanical Colour at your Fingertips*. Available in print and as an eBook.

rebeccadesnos.com

Introducing the contributors...

Louise Upshall is an eco-printer and natural dyer living in the beautiful Blue Mountains of Australia. She loves teaching her methods of eco-printing through ebooks, ecourses and workshops. Her latest offering is the Iso Dye Club, a "use what you have, pay what you can" ecourse designed to help people connect with plants, creativity and community from home. To eco-print with leaves, follow Louise's tutorial on page 21. *gumnutmagic.com*

Samorn Sanixay is a weaver, textile designer and passionate gardener. Samorn is the cofounder of Eastern Weft, a weaving cooperative based in Vientiane, Laos, which supports disadvantaged young Hill Tribe women through art and weaving. Samorn's brand new leaf and flower pounding tutorial is on page 35. *easternweft.com*

Yasuna Iman is an artist who creates abstract compositions on paper using self-made botanical pigments alongside blind tree drawings. Her work explores the versatility of plants, their organic properties, aesthetic qualities, and symbolic value. Born in Paris, she lives and works in Berlin. On page 47, Yasuna shares tips for creating a blind drawing, then shows us how to make ink from pine cones. *yasunaiman.com*

Flora Arbuthnott is a UK-based natural dyer, grower, and forager who connects with the land through developing relationships with plants and fungi. Flora explores wild and cultivated plants to produce a variety of vibrant colours. Flora runs a selection of natural dye workshops and ecourses. Read about Flora's dye garden on page 65 where you can find some tips for starting your own garden. *floraarbuthnott.com*

Tina Bettison is a writer and photographer with a passion for growing plants from cuttings for her garden in rural Nottinghamshire in the UK. Growing up with green-fingered parents, she is carrying on the tradition of making plant-based memories and gardening as self care. On page 73, Tina shares tips for growing plants from cuttings. *tinabettisonwordsmith.com*

Maggie Pate is the designer and purveyor of Nåde Studio. She began her career in fashion modelling internationally then retired to work for a clothing label in New York City. With a deep connection to nature, she reversed her career to focus on sustainability and textiles. Maggie's dye book is called *The Natural Colors Cookbook* and she has a series of online classes and home dye kits. Follow Maggie's tutorial on page 77 to bundle dye your own scarf with flowers. *nade-studio.com*

Tricia Paoluccio is a professional actor and creative from California, living in New York City with her husband and two sons. She has worked on Broadway, in television and film, currently in Hunters on Amazon Prime and the upcoming Plot Against America. Her work with pressed flowers has attracted numerous fashion designers and companies in New York City and she will be sharing the results of these collaborations soon. Tricia shares some flower pressing tips on page 95. *modernpressedflower.com*

Safety notes *(Please read further guidelines on page 105)*

- Take care when identifying plants and if you need guidance, consult a reliable book or a knowledgeable friend.
- Use a separate set of equipment reserved for dyeing – not your kitchen pots etc.
- Keep dyes away from children, pets and food.
- When you are heating dye pots, make sure you have good air flow. Keep a window open and don't stand over a steaming pot and breathe in the vapour.
- Wear gloves to protect your skin.

11

21

35

47

55

85

73

77

28

65

Contents

95

botanical inks on paper

Let's harness the natural gifts from plants and make our own botanical inks. I'll show you how to make yellow ink from pomegranate skins and a peachy-pink from avocado stones, then alter the pH levels to expand the range of shades.

Words and photos by Rebecca Desnos

Never toss these stones or skins into the compost or bin again! You can simply simmer them in water to extract beautiful colours, then use the dye as watercolour paints. We're essentially making a mini dye pot of super concentrated dye. The key is to use as little water as possible so the colour is strong, whilst ensuring that the plant matter doesn't dry out and burn. Although this method is simple, don't feel tempted to multitask in the kitchen as your dye pot needs your close attention.

What you need

- 6 avocado stones: Hass avocados give the pinkest shades.
- Skins from 2 pomegranates. The variety with yellow on the inside of the skins is the most promising for dye potential.
- Small-medium saucepan with a lid
- Wooden spoon
- Sieve
- Bowl
- Old piece of muslin cloth for straining
- Lidded jars for storing ink
- Rubber gloves
- Optional: cloves or a couple of drops of wintergreen essential oil to preserve your ink

It is advisable to keep a separate set of dye equipment and not use your kitchen items. These particular dye plants may come from fruit, but the skins and stones themselves are not edible. You could downgrade an old kitchen pot and wooden spoon to use exclusively for dyeing from now on, or pick up some cheap items in a charity shop. In the photos, I use an aluminium pot, which is the kind of pot I use for most of my dyeing. Aluminium is not recommended for cooking food as the metal is reactive and contaminates food. However, this feature can be helpful for dyeing: the metal reacts with the dye particles, brightens shades and also helps the colour last longer in sunlight.

Safety

*   Please read the safety guidelines on page 105.
*   Label jars of ink clearly when storing in the fridge.

Collecting your dye plants

*   Avocados: Wash and freeze the avocado stones as you eat the avocados, or use fresh.
*   Pomegranates: Either use the skins fresh, or dry for future use. To dry: wash the skins then allow them to air dry. Store in a paper bag – they keep like this for years.

PLANT DYE ZINE

Making pomegranate skin ink

1. Break the skins into smaller pieces and drop into your dye pot.

2. Cover with just enough water so that the skins are submerged.

3. Put the lid on and heat gently for 20 minutes. Gentle heat is ideal as it helps keep the colours bright. The aim is to coax out the colour, rather than cook the skins aggressively. Top up the water level as needed, so the pot doesn't dry out and burn.

4. After heating for 30 minutes, turn off the heat and keep the lid on. Allow the skins to soak in the hot water for a few hours and the dye will intensify in colour.

5. You may choose to heat again for another 15-20 minutes to coax out more colour.

6. Control the concentration of the dye by simmering away more liquid.

7. When you're satisfied with the depth of colour, strain the dye into a bowl by pouring through a sieve lined with a cloth. The cloth will catch finer particles of plant matter and you will be left with a beautifully clear liquid. Pour into a jar, add a couple of cloves or drops of wintergreen essential oil. Then label clearly and refrigerate.

Making avocado stone ink

1. Drop your avocado stones into your dye pot and fill with water – just enough to cover the stones.

2. Put the lid on and heat gently for 30 minutes. Keep a close eye on the pot and top up the water as needed. Gentle heat is essential, as aggressive heat can turn your dye brown.

3. Turn off the heat and allow the water to cool.

4. The stones will have softened by now, so try to carefully break them apart with your wooden spoon. Some stones will easily split in two and others might shatter into smaller pieces. We want to expose the inside of the stones to extract more dye.

5. Heat again for 30 minutes on low heat. Remember the aim is to gently coax out the colour – not to cook the plants. Allow some water to evaporate so the dye becomes more concentrated.

6. Allow the dye pot to sit for several hours. This gives the dye the chance to oxidise further. It may become pinker at this point, or stay a peachy-pink shade.

7. Strain out the stones through a sieve lined with a muslin cloth into a bowl.

8. When you're happy with the colour, pour it into a jar. Add a couple of cloves (or drops of wintergreen essential oil) to help it stay fresh, label the jar and store in the fridge.

Avocado dye tips

- Avocado skins also make beautiful pink shades. The skins store well when dried. Before drying, make sure you scrape out any remaining green flesh and wash thoroughly. Leave to air dry, then keep in a paper bag.

- The dye colours vary depending on the variety of avocados and the time of year. If your dye is more beige than peach, allow the skins or stones to sit in the dye pot for longer and see if a pinker shade develops as the dye oxidises.

- In general, increasing the pH of avocado dye will shift it towards a pinker tone. I'll show you how to do this on the following pages.

- Your tap water will also affect the final shade. Compare tap water, rain water and sea water to see if you get different shades.

avocado stones +
bicarbonate of soda

avocado stones

pomegranate skins

pomegranate skins +
bicarbonate of soda

Altering the pH levels

Most plant dyes are pH sensitive which means they will react to acids and alkalis. Both of the dyes we have made darken considerably when bicarbonate of soda (baking soda) is added. When you decide to paint with your dyes, pour a small amount into a bowl or palette. Then sprinkle a tiny amount of bicarbonate of soda into the ink and stir with your paint brush. You should see an immediate change in colour and you can paint with it straight away. Interestingly, the ink in the palette continues to darken over the course of the day.

Painting with your inks

- Use your ink just as you would watercolour paint.
- Colours from plants can be quite subtle yet dynamic. If you paint at night, you might be shocked that the colours seem very dull, but they will come to life in the daylight.
- Some inks will dry darker which is often a surprise. For example, a pale yellow pomegranate skin dye can oxidise on paper and result in a neon yellow.
- Mix dye colours together in a paint palette to build a wider range of shades. Avocado stone ink combines well with the yellow from pomegranate skins to make orange.
- It's fun to experiment with thickening inks into a paint consistency. Simmer your dye and add in a small amount of powdered gum, whilst whisking until you reach a good consistency. For detailed instructions, go to page 55.

How long do dyes last in the fridge?

The inks should stay fresh in the fridge for a few weeks. Whole cloves or wintergreen essential oil will help keep the dyes fresher for longer. Experiment with adding in drops of other essential oils that are naturally antibacterial and antifungal. Discard your inks if they go mouldy.

Alternatively, pour the dye into ice cube trays and freeze, as shown on page 53.

How long do the colours last?

Pomegranate skins: The presence of tannins means that it has excellent colourfastness properties and it actually darkens slightly in sunlight.

Avocado stones: If your ink is particularly pink, then the colour is likely to dull in sunlight and end up more of a peachy shade.

Before creating any artwork with these inks, test the light fastness by painting a small piece of paper then cutting it in half. Put one half in the sunlight for a couple of weeks and keep the other half in a dark place. After two weeks, compare the two swatches and see how much the colour has changed.

Modifying dyes with iron

You can use iron water or ferrous sulphate to darken these colours. To use ferrous sulphate, follow the steps on page 32. Pink avocado dye shifts to greyish-purple and yellow pomegranate skin dye turns greenish-brown!

eco-printing with leaves

Louise Upshall shows us how to revive a
well-worn item of clothing by printing it with leaves.

*Words and photos
by Louise Upshall, Gumnut Magic*

Eco-printing is a type of natural dyeing that creates leaf prints on fabric. Natural dyeing usually involves creating a dye bath and letting the fabric float freely, so that it picks up a solid layer of colour. With eco-printing, the leaves or other dyestuff are placed directly on the fabric, which is then rolled or folded up, tied tightly and heated. The heat releases the colour just where each leaf is touching the fabric and so you get leaf-shaped prints.

Not only does this create a beautiful and very unique result, but it also has some advantages over traditional dyeing methods. You can do it in a smaller dye pot, because you create a tight bundle rather than needing lots of space for the fabric to move freely. This means less energy is required to heat the pot. You also use less plant material for the same amount of fabric. And different leaves will give different results, so you can very easily create multiple colours, shades and shapes on one piece. This also makes it a wonderful method for freshening up a beloved but worn out item of clothing, or to cover up stains.

Usually eco-printing requires scouring and mordanting the fabric, and sometimes preparing the leaves in different ways. Here I share a simpler, more accessible method to get you started.

1. Make a simple mordant

Mordants are metallic salts that help plant dyes bond with fabric. There's no need to buy powdered mordants, which come packaged in plastic and are a health hazard to breathe in.

Instead, make a simple iron mordant by gathering some scrap pieces of rusty metal. Place them in a jar and cover with white vinegar. Your mordant is ready to use once the vinegar has started to change colour, although it will keep getting more potent. This can take several weeks. Each time you use it, top it up with more vinegar to keep it acidic.

2. Choose a well-worn item of clothing

Choose a piece of clothing to eco-print. You can use any plant-based fibre such as cotton, linen, or even viscose. I've demonstrated on a top, but the same process can be used for dresses, skirts, trousers and pieces of cloth. If it's fabric and you can roll it up, then it can be eco-printed.

Use something which you already have in your wardrobe, or look at your local second-hand store. In addition to the ecological benefits of upcycling, well-washed fabric actually absorbs natural dyes better. You can use a white or lightly coloured item and it doesn't matter if there are a few stains. These will be covered up in the dyeing process or become a beautiful part of the final design.

3. Go on a leaf-gathering walk

Wander through your garden or neighbourhood gathering leaves. Bring mindfulness and attention to this process.

Pick the leaves respectfully and don't take more than you need.

For this top, I have used rose and geranium leaves. Some other reliable eco-printing plants include maple, eucalyptus and blackberry. Or you could simply pick a leaf from each tree you pass and see what happens.

4. How to eco-print your clothing

When your mordant is ready, and you have gathered an item of clothing and some leaves, you are ready to eco-print.

Gather your materials

- Iron mordant
- Big handful of fresh leaves
- Cotton top or other clothing item
- Plastic gloves or tweezers
- Piece of scrap cotton to use as a wrapping cloth
- String, wool, yarn or strips of old cotton
- Small dye pot

Safety notes

Please read the safety guidelines on page 105. Ensure that you use a separate pot for dyeing – not your kitchen equipment.

Caring for your creation

All dyes, not just natural, will eventually fade. Harsh detergents and sunlight accelerate this process. So wash your eco-printed garment with a mild detergent and dry it in the shade. When the leaf prints do fade, enjoy the process of gathering more leaves and re-printing the clothing.

1. Soak your leaves in the iron mordant for about 5 minutes. Then remove them and let them dry to avoid mordant spots on your fabric. Wear plastic gloves or use tweezers for this process, to avoid touching the mordant with bare skin.

2. Lay your item of clothing front side down. Cover the back of the clothing with leaves (some facing up and some facing down). Lay out your wrapping cloth at the end of your clothing, and cover with some extra leaves to roll onto.

3. Start rolling up the clothing. As you roll, notice how the front of the clothing is now coming into contact with the leaves you have placed on the back. In this way, you get prints from both sides of each leaf.

4. Roll onto the wrapping cloth, making sure there are enough extra leaves to make contact with the remaining front of the clothing.

5. Completely wrap the clothing up, folding the sides of the wrapping cloth onto the bundle.

6. Wrap up your bundle with string, squeezing it tightly with the other hand. You want to achieve a firm pressure so that all of the leaves are making contact with the fabric. This will help you get clear prints.

7. Put the tied up bundle in your dye pot and cover with boiling water. Simmer for about 1 hour, then allow to cool.

8. Unwrap your bundle and delight in the prints left by the leaves. The colours of nature are infused in the fabric. Rinse out your string, clothing and wrapping cloth.

petal paint

Explore your local flowers by turning petals into watercolour paints.

Words and photos by Rebecca Desnos

This is such a simple and beautiful way to sample local dye colours. All you need is hot water and a little bowl. If you take a thermos flask of hot water, you can even do this when you're outside in nature and paint on the go! I've used dried flowers from my African violet house plant, as well as marigolds and coreopsis from my balcony. This technique works best with deeply pigmented flowers.

What you need:

- Flowers (fresh or dried)
- A few little bowls (do not use for food again afterwards) or little jars with lids (helpful when travelling)
- A stick
- Lemon juice or vinegar
- Bicarbonate of soda (baking soda)
- Paintbrushes
- Paper for painting
- Optional: sieve and paint palette

Safety: Please take care when identifying flowers and ensure that they are not toxic. Follow the safety guidelines on page 105.

Let's make our paint!

1. Pick off the petals from a few deeply pigmented flowers and drop into a bowl or glass jar. Pour a little hot water over the petals – just enough so the petals are covered. Mix well with the stick (or the end of a paintbrush) and try to squash the petals to extract more colour. Leave for a little while to allow the colour to darken.

2. When you're happy with the depth of colour, you can just dip your brush into the liquid and begin painting. Or strain out the petals to leave a clear paint that's free of any petals.

3. The dye from petals is often pH sensitive, so pour a little dye into a couple of the wells in a paint palette (or extra bowls) and add a squeeze of lemon juice or vinegar to one, and a sprinkle of bicarbonate of soda to another. If the dye is pH sensitive, the colours are likely to change immediately. As you paint, rinse your paintbrush between dips so you don't contaminate the pH of each liquid.

African Violet

African Violet + lemon

African Violet + baking soda

Coreopsis

Coreopsis + lemon

Coreopsis + baking soda

Red Marigold

Most flowers dry well. Store in paper envelopes in a dry place. Then simply add hot water and stir to release colour.

Coreopsis
+ lemon juice

Coreopsis
+ baking soda

Coreopsis

Coreopsis

This is one of my favourite flowers for making petal paint. I've been growing a variety called Early Sunrise on my balcony for a few years. It flowers from early spring to late summer. There are countless varieties of coreopsis – some are grown as annuals and some as perennials – and as far as I know, they all give dye. The blooms are bursting with colour, so just a handful of petals goes a long way.

Do the colours last?

The colours from some flowers will last longer than others, so bare this in mind when creating art. I was pleasantly surprised by how well the colour on these paintings lasted.

To test light fastness, paint a piece of paper then cover it partially with a piece of thick card. Leave it in the sunlight for a few weeks and then peek under the cardboard to check for fading.

Painting fabric

Follow the method on page 104 to see how to pretreat your fabric in soya (soy) milk, and go to page 62 to thicken your dye into a paint consistency. This thickened paint can be used on fabric or paper. Enjoy experimenting!

Early Sunrise Coreopsis

Modifying colours with iron

Let's take things a step further now and widen our range of colours with iron. Iron is commonly used in natural dyeing to darken dyes and improve colourfastness. You can make your own iron mordant by following the recipe on page 22, or you can buy a small packet of ferrous sulphate crystals. One packet will last for years, as we only use a tiny sprinkle each time.

Safety: Please wear gloves whilst working with iron as it irritates the skin (thin, clear gloves allow good dexterity for painting). Follow the safety guidelines on page 105.

These are a few ways that we can use iron to modify our dyes.

1. Darken the dye

Pour a small amount of your petal paint into a new bowl, then sprinkle the tiniest amount of ferrous sulphate crystals into the dye. The colour will darken instantly. Stir with your paintbrush and begin painting.

If you are using your homemade iron mordant, simply pour a small amount into the petal paint and see if there's a colour change. The colour change may not be as dramatic, because your homemade iron mordant may not be as concentrated as ferrous sulphate crystals.

Keep a separate paintbrush for iron-darkened paints, so you don't accidentally contaminate brighter dyes and turn these a muddy colour.

2. Make patterns

Now we will use iron water to create darker patterns on our paintings. First we need to make up a bowl of iron mordant, then we can simply paint this onto our flower paintings.

If you are using homemade iron water, simply pour a small amount into a bowl and paint with this directly onto your paintings. Watch the petal colours darken immediately.

Or make an iron mordant with ferrous sulphate crystals. Pour a small amount of water into a bowl and sprinkle in a few ferrous sulphate crystals. Mix with your paintbrush and watch the liquid turn a rusty orange colour. Now use this liquid to paint directly onto your paintings and see the shades change.

Try painting onto wet paint, as well as wet on dry. See the different effects you can create.

3. Sprinkle ferrous sulphate crystals

It's as simple as it sounds! Wearing gloves to protect your skin, sprinkle ferrous sulphate crystals onto a wet painting and see darker speckles emerge. Some areas will bleed into others. It's an unpredictable and exciting way to make patterns. Allow the paintings to dry then dust or scrape off the crystals.

Orange and yellow shades were
made from coreopsis flowers.
Green, purple and grey/blue come
from purple pincushion flowers.

flower + leaf pounding

Samorn Sanixay shares a brand new plant hammering tutorial with us. Find out how to preserve the colours and intricate patterns from flowers and leaves on fabric.

Words & tutorial by Samorn Sanixay
Photos by Graeme Smith (peonypress.com.au)

History & inspiration

Leaf hammering or pounding is a process of transferring pigment from flowers and leaves to fabric by using a hammer or mallet. The hammer can be made of metal, rubber or wood as long as it has a flat surface. This technique can transfer flowers or leaves onto cloth so detailed it can look like a watercolour painting. It's a great way to preserve the colours of summer or a special bloom. The pieces you create can be included in quilting projects, cushions or framed art.

It is unknown exactly when and where this technique originated. However, the Silk Road may have contributed to its distribution, with its ancient network of trade routes that linked China to the West. Over centuries, traders exchanged new exotic fibres, textiles, patterns and colours, along with new techniques. Local ethnic groups across the world have adopted this technique to their local surroundings. For example, in Indonesia they use young Indian almond and teak leaves to create spectacular red prints.

Studying culture in textiles allows us to understand how various groups of people have contributed to the development of textile art and the technology required to produce the works.

Many years ago when I was experimenting with new ideas for patchwork, I began researching quilt patterns around the world and came across the work of a lady named Bettye Kimbrell (1936 - 2016). She was a quilter from Alabama and when I read her story it reminded me of my own grandmother back in her village in Laos. Bettye and my grandmother both grew up in poverty in different ways but were self sufficient where they relied entirely off their land for food and clothing.

Bettye was taught stitching and quilting by her grandmother and later went on to design her own patterns. One day she came across beautiful flower and leaf pounded quilts at a quilting fair. She became fascinated by this technique which was inspired by Native American Cherokee people.

When I learnt that Bettye had passed away in 2016, I decided to explore this technique further to continue and honour her story and my grandmother at the same time. After repeated experiments with various tools and materials, the following are my own results, keeping things as simple as possible for you to try at home. The leaves and flowers used are what was available in my garden on the day.

Method

I use this technique when there are flowers, leaves and petals in the garden but there aren't enough to extract colour in a dye pot. So the next best thing is to preserve them intact, as a print, just as you see them. Sometimes the result is even better than the flower or leaf because there may be some patterns and colours hidden that the naked eye is unable to see. There is also an element of surprise where a completely different colour appears after pounding.

This technique is also a fun introduction for children to learn and appreciate nature and the art of natural dyes where the results are instant.

You can choose any flower or leaf that is in your garden, or go for a walk in your neighbourhood. This could be a chance to meet new people, make new friends but most of all discover the beauty of plants in your local area.

There are so many plants in different climates that I haven't personally tried, so test your local flora to see which ones work for you. *Only gather plants that you can identify and are not toxic.*

In general, I have found that most dark flowers work best for this technique and yellow flowers eventually fade. It is best to choose leaves that are dark green in colour and are soft. For this reason, eucalyptus leaves will not work for this technique as they are too hard. Make sure the leaves are fresh and moist. If you want to save your leaves, place them between two paper towels and store in a paper bag and lay them flat in the fridge

Since I wrote the original tutorial in 2017, I have kept a detailed catalogue and observed which plants stood the test of time over the three year period.

On the opposite page is a list of recommended flowers and plants. Please note that leaves contain chlorophyll which is the green pigment in their cells. For this technique we are transferring the pigment onto cloth. All chlorophyll is living, and as it dies, so does the green colour. Most of these leaves will fade to a khaki colour, like an antique piece revealing veins and lifelines.

Tried + tested plants

These are some of the plants that I like to use, but I encourage you to explore your local flora and discover many more plants that work well with this pounding technique!

Flowers: poppy, evening primrose, aquilegia/columbine (purples) buddleia, dahlias, red rose petals, salvia, cyclamen, marigold, cosmos, coreopsis.

Leaves: maple leaves of all varieties, rose, geranium, aquilegia/columbine, blueberry, avocado, tomato, indigo leaves, lemon balm, sage, parsley, red vein sorrel, salvia, poppy leaves, chamomile, hydrangea, pineapple sage, amaranthus, fern, gingko, honeysuckle, hickory.

silk

cotton calico

linen

Materials needed

For this method, thick cotton or linen fabric works best. It is also possible to create these effects on art paper.

If you want to mordant or pretreat fabric, follow the soya milk directions on page 104. You can also presoak fabric in a bucket of vinegar solution made from 1 part vinegar and 3 parts water. Leave for 30 minutes before removing and allow to dry.

What you need

- Two pieces of cotton or linen fabric, or one piece folded in half.
- Medium sized mallet or hammer. A few examples are shown in the photo below.
- Large wooden board or cardboard placed underneath fabric. Never place fabric directly onto concrete as you will create holes in the fabric.

For flowers: before starting, tear flower petals with your fingers to see if the colour stains. If not, there will be no colour on the fabric.

A note on the weather: This technique is best done on a sunny or dry day as many tests have been done the day after rain with disappointing results. The flowers and leaves bleed and become diluted as a result of drinking too much water.

Instructions - part 1

1. Gather all the materials and tools you wish to use. I've used three types of fabric - silk, cotton and linen - to show different results.

2. Place the fabric onto the wooden board.

3. Lay your leaves and petals onto the fabric.

4. Cover the piece of fabric, leaves and petals with another piece of cotton so that when you pound the leaves, it will protect your work. Or fold your fabric in half, so one side covers the other.

5. Pound each leaf under the cotton to reveal the print.

6. Keep going until you have finished with the desired look. You will have a print on both pieces of fabric.

7. Unfold or remove the top fabric to see the results. Leave to dry for at least 24 hours.

8. Shake to remove the dried petals and leaves, then iron to seal the dye and colour. The heat and metal of the iron helps with colourfastness and enhancing the prints.

Part 2

Since the first tutorial was written back in 2017, some further experiments have been done to test colourfastness of the cloth with some very good results.

If you would like to take things a step further, or instantly change the effects of the pounding technique, here are a few methods to try. **Safety**: follow the guidelines on page 105, and most importantly, do not use your cooking pots.

Boiling

After pounding, allow the fabric to dry.

Fill a pot with 1 litre of water and allow the water to boil. Once the water begins to boil, turn off the heat and drop the cloth in the water and leave it in there for around 30 minutes. *(Photo A)*

Remove the fabric and leave to dry. You may notice some of the green prints have been enhanced. Then iron the fabric.

Steaming

Place the fabric in a steamer for at least 20 minutes. Keep the lid on to keep the steam in the pot. Interestingly, steaming often changes red pigments to blue. I found there was a significantly higher chance of flowers retaining their colour after steaming as opposed to simply pounding and leaving the fabric to dry. *(Photo B)*

A

B

C

E

D

Bundling and boiling

Here we will use metal rods as we do in other bundle dyeing methods. Find a small metal rod that will fit into your dye pot.

1. Place the rod at the edge of the fabric.

2. Spray vinegar over the pounded fabric - enough to dampen. (Photo C)

3. Roll the fabric and metal rod all the way to the end. (Photo D)

4. Use a piece of string and wrap around the fabric to secure it tightly. This will be going into a pot of boiling water. (Photo E)

5. Place the bundle into a pot of water and boil for at least 30 minutes. *(Photo F)*

6. Remove the bundle and allow it to cool for several minutes before unravelling to see your results. *(Photos G + H)*. Different metals will give a range of results similar to when using metallic salts as mordants, but rods are less toxic.

7. Allow all the pieces of fabric to dry. You can rinse or iron the fabric for final results to see which plants and leaves worked best and marvel at your works of art.

A final note: There is no right or wrong – it is a matter of opinion and taste for the results. I encourage you to never give up and keep exploring as there are always surprises!

F

G

H

The results...

silk

linen

Pounded, then steamed for 30 minutes. Allowed to dry, then ironed.

cotton calico

linen

cotton calico

Pounded and then rolled around a copper rod and boiled for 40 minutes. Unravelled, rinsed, dried and ironed.

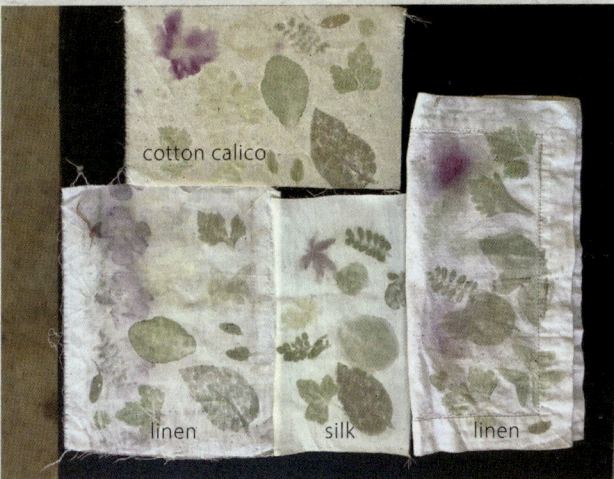

cotton calico

linen

silk

linen

Fabric was pounded, then rolled around an iron rod. Boiled for 40 minutes, then allowed to cool and dried. It was then put through a 35 minute wash at 40°C, dried, then ironed.

Photos on page 45 are by Samorn Sanixay

inspiration from the forest

Experience the forest, create blind drawings of trees and paint with pinecones.

Words by Yasuna Iman

Photos by Johannes Berger
instagram.com/jhnsberger

"...I INSTINCTIVELY COMBINED BLIND TREE DRAWING WITH PLANT PIGMENT MAKING AND FOUND SOLACE WITNESSING THIS ORGANIC ENCOUNTER."

Eyes wide open, I could see the crown of elms and ashes, tilting to one side and the other, as the wind blew through their bodies. The branches could have been their arms and they held each other's hands while their heads were floating above mine. I watched their slow and silent dance for about a minute, and without looking at the blank page lying on my knees, I took a deep breath and drew the first line.

This has happened many times since then. Still, every single blind line I draw carries in itself the essence of the first ones and of the way they appeared to me. I had lost my way walking in the forest, and my former steps already disappeared from the soil when I realised I couldn't find them anymore. My field of vision began to fill with an overwhelming myriad of lines, which were as many roots, trunks, branches and twigs tightly tangled around me. This scene took my breath away, to replace it with the thought that I wouldn't find my way back.

Lost in this maze of lines from trees, I started losing track of time as well. After a while, I surrendered and eventually sat on a log that seemed asleep under moss covers. With my eyes following the intricate curves of the birch standing in front of me, I instinctively reached for

my journal folded in my pocket, found a pencil, a blank page, and started drawing. My gaze moved across the trees at the same pace as my hand on the invisible piece of paper, as if they were the ones holding the pencil, or if I was drawing with my sight alone. When I finally looked at the page, I discovered these lines that looked nothing like trees, yet felt deeply right.

I wasn't searching for anything anymore, still, lost in this forest, it seemed I found something.

Shortly after, I discovered the realm of natural dyes and couldn't stop painting with plants I would find just about anywhere. Diving deeper into these botanical experiments, I instinctively combined blind tree drawing with plant pigment making and found solace witnessing this organic encounter. The more I was in nature, the more I created, and as inspiration grew, I longed for nature. I've been blissfully spinning in this virtuous circle ever since.

I now find lines and colours in the forest and purposefully lose myself among trees. I watch their slow and silent dance for about a minute, and without looking at the blank page lying on my knees, I take a deep breath and draw the first line.

Blind drawing

The idea behind blind tree drawing is to pay attention to your sensations and release any expectations of the outcome. Try this intuitive exercise with nothing more than a piece of paper, a pencil, and a tree.

On a forest walk, find a comfortable spot. Take a moment to connect with your surroundings without drawing yet. Observe the trees, their lines, their curves. Only then, start drawing the line that your eyes are following, without looking at the paper, nor aiming for accuracy. Then draw the next line. Meanwhile, take in smells and sounds, feel your breath, take your time. Continue until you feel ready to discover your drawing.

"OBSERVE THE TREES, THEIR LINES, THEIR CURVES."

These dyes are from blueberries (green) and elderberries (purple).

Pinecone paint

Now imagine that after drawing, you collected some pinecones on the way home. Once you arrive back home, you can create a natural paint from them and maybe, add it to your drawing.

Here's a simple recipe to try (please first read the safety notes on page 105):

- Place the pinecones in a saucepan and pour in enough water to cover them. A little water goes a long way, so no need to submerge them.
- Heat the liquid gently then let it simmer until you're satisfied with the colour.
- Turn off the stove but leave the saucepan on the burner until it cools down. Water will further evaporate, allowing the pigment to deepen and thicken.
- Strain the liquid through a sieve and transfer to a smaller container to paint from.
- Pour any leftovers into an ice cube tray and store in the freezer. Later, simply release some watercolour cubes and let them melt to reuse the paint.

Try this technique with other cones, such as alder and redwood. The colours will all be slightly different shades of brown, with varying degrees of warmth.

Tip

Pour any excess dye into an ice cube tray and freeze for future painting sessions. As with all equipment you use for dyeing, don't use for food again. These dyes are made from black tea (top), elderberries (lower right) and eucalyptus (left).

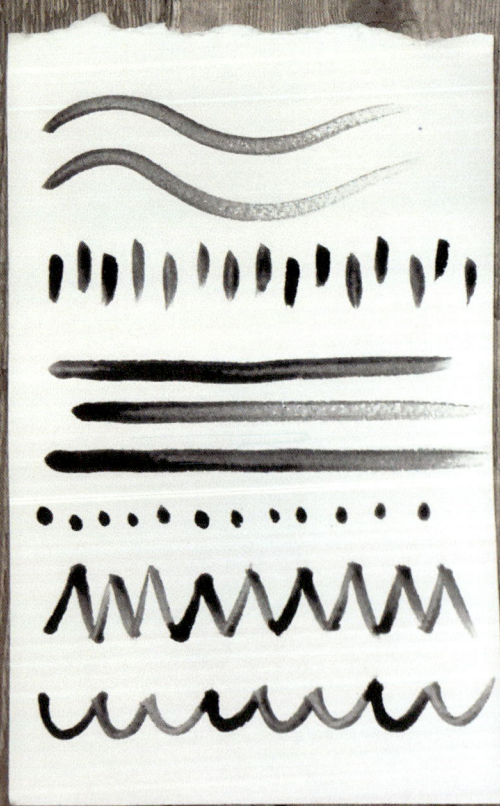

making paint from oak galls

Did you know that you can make black dye from oak galls and iron? Just a small handful of oak galls contains enough tannins to make a jar of paint. I'll show you how to thicken dye into the consistency of paint which is perfect for printing or painting. The black is incredibly colourfast and the creative possibilities are endless!

You can use this method with any dye plant and I'll show you how to adapt the recipe very slightly to make paint from coreopsis flowers. Then you will be able to make paint from any dye plant that you have at your fingertips!

Words and photos by Rebecca Desnos

What are oak galls?

Oak galls, also known as gall nuts or oak apples, are small swellings found on oak trees and are particularly useful for natural dyeing as they are exceptionally high in tannins. Gall wasps lay eggs on young shoots of oak trees and the tree reacts to the invasion by growing new plant material around the larvae. A hard round ball is produced – the oak gall – which becomes the larvae's home. When we collect oak galls from branches, little holes can be clearly seen which shows us that the wasp has emerged.

The tannins in oak galls can be easily extracted in water and the high tannin content reacts with iron in a spectacular way to produce black dye. There is a long history of oak galls being used to make writing ink.

Tip for collecting oak galls

Wasps lay eggs on new branches, so look out for young oak trees which have low branches. This is where I've had the most success finding them. If you haven't had luck spotting any, you can buy gall nut extract from some natural dye supply websites.

Alternatively, make a paler grey dye from other sources of tannin such as acorns, oak leaves and bark. These contain lower levels of tannins than oak galls, so you will need larger quantities of plant matter for a dark shade. If you don't have oak trees near you, try other sources of tannin, such as black tea and pomegranate skins.

Materials

- Approx. 10g oak galls (or a small handful of what you can find)
- 2 cups of water
- ½ teaspoon ferrous sulphate crystals
- ¾ teaspoon gum tragacanth, which can be bought from cake decorating or herbal shops
- Fabric, cushion covers or clothing made from natural fibres, e.g. cotton, linen, hemp. Note that iron will eventually eat through animal protein fibres, such as wool and silk.

Tools

- Old pillowcase and hammer
- Stainless steel pot (don't use aluminium as you will be adding iron into the pot and it will react with the aluminium and potentially contaminate all future dyes)
- Wooden stirring spoon
- Sieve & muslin cloth for straining
- A bowl for straining into
- ½ cup and ¼ tsp measures
- Paintbrush and/or vegetables cut into shapes to use as stamps
- Piece of plastic or an old plastic lid to use as a paint tray
- Large piece of card cut to the same size as your clothing or cushion cover to slip inside, to prevent paint from bleeding through the layers
- Gloves to protect your skin

Safety

Please read the safety guidelines on page 105, and most importantly don't use your kitchen pots for dyeing.

Method

1. Wash your fabric in the washing machine, then follow the soya milk instructions on page 104 then wait a week before painting fabric. Or mordant in another way.

2. Put your oak galls into an old pillowcase (or bundled up in an old tea towel) and carefully crush them with a hammer. Continue until the pieces are small.

3. Add the crushed oak galls into your dye pot and cover with two cups of water. *(photo A)*

4. Simmer for 30 minutes. You can allow the water to evaporate a little, but top up the water as necessary so the galls don't burn.

5. Allow the oak galls to soak in the water for as long as you like. This will further intensify the tannin content of the liquid.

6. After a few hours, or days (if you're busy), strain the liquid through a cloth to catch all the little pieces. I like to line a metal sieve with an old muslin cloth. *(photo B)*

7. You can save the soggy oak gall pieces and spread them onto a piece of card and let them dry. Store the dry pieces in a paper bag for a future dyeing session.

8. Wipe your dye pot clean and pour the dye back in there.

9. Next we will add ferrous sulphate which will react with the tannins

A

B

and turn the dye black. Add ½ teaspoon of ferrous sulphate crystals to your dye. It doesn't matter if the dye is warm or cold at this stage. The colour will darken immediately. Keep stirring until the crystals have fully dissolved. *(photo C)*

10. At this point you can do several things with your dye:
    - Thicken with a gum to make paint, which we will do next.
    - Dye wooden beads black in this concentrated dye.
    - Dilute with water and dye clothing. Diluting the dye will produce a paler grey shade.
    - Add gum arabic and use as a writing or painting ink.

11. Measure the remaining volume of dye. For each cup of liquid, you need approximately ¾ teaspoon of gum tragacanth. Reheat the dye in your dye pot, and sprinkle in the gum tragacanth powder. Stir continuously to dissolve it fully. Watch as the dye thickens. It will thicken even more as it cools.

12. Take a spare piece of fabric and paint a line *(photo D)*. We are looking for a crisp line that doesn't bleed. If the colour bleeds, add a little more gum tragacanth, then paint another line to see if it is crisper. Adjust the thickness of the paint to get the desired result. (My paint was just right with ¾ tsp. gum tragacanth for 1 cup of dye).

13. Pour your paint into a jar, label it, and keep in the fridge until you're ready to use it.

14. When you paint fabric, you may find that the fabric drags with the brush and paint bleeds through to the bottom layer. A simple solution is to place a piece of cardboard inside your t-shirt or cushion cover, between the layers of fabric. Draw around your t-shirt on a piece of cardboard, cut out, and slip inside. If your t-shirt is really stretchy, cut the cardboard a little bit bigger so the fabric is slightly stretched. You can tape a single piece of fabric to the table so it doesn't slip around, or put a smaller piece into an embroidery hoop.

15. Think about the design you'd like to create on the fabric, and test on a scrap of fabric first to get the feel for how the paint transfers onto the cloth with a brush or stamp. You may need to go over the pattern a second time to fill in paler areas. Experiment with more or less paint to get different effects. When you're feeling confident, paint or print your final piece of fabric or clothing.

16. Finish your design on the front of your top or cushion. Allow the paint to dry before you turn over and paint the back. When you have finished, hang it up to dry.

17. Next, we will set the dye with a hot iron. Iron over the print on the hottest heat that the type of fabric can handle.

18. Now put your fabric on a cycle in the washing machine – ideally use a natural laundry detergent. This will wash out any traces of iron. Note: other dyes benefit from waiting a few days before washing. This can help the fabric retain more colour, but this isn't such a problem with oak galls as the dye is so potent.

19. As oak gall dye is very colourfast, you can wear and wash as you do your other clothing. The colour may fade to a dark grey on some types of fabric. When you use this method with other plant dyes, you will need to take further precautions such keeping out of the direct sunlight.

Further experiments

Other gums to try include guar gum and acacia gum (gum arabic). These will require different quantities to thicken to the desired texture.

You can use this simple method with any kind of plant that is rich in tannins. The principle is very simple: simmer the plant matter in water, strain, then add ferrous sulphate to darken.

Every plant will produce slightly different shades when it interacts with iron. Experiment with different plants and see! To get you started, I'll show you how to make coreopsis paint on the following page.

*Background fabric was
dyed with avocado
stones and iron to
make grey-purple.*

Coreopsis flower paint

I used the same method as for the oak gall paint, but heated the coreopsis flowers more gently to keep their vibrant shade. If we boil flowers, it can turn the dye brown. I used a smaller dye pot this time, as I used less water. The aim is to end up with a highly concentrated dye. Remember to pretreat your fabric in soya milk, by following the steps on page 104, (or mordant in another way).

Materials

- a handful of coreopsis petals (dried or fresh is fine)
- half a cup of water
- gum tragacanth

Method

1. Simmer the petals in half a cup of water for a couple of minutes and stir regularly. Then leave the petals to sit in the dye pot for a while longer (minimum of an hour, but it can be as long as you like). Stir regularly to encourage the dye to extract into the water.

2. When you are happy with the colour of your dye, strain the petals through a sieve lined with a piece of muslin (or other fine fabric).

3. Wipe the pot clean, then pour half of the remaining dye into a bowl and set aside. We will darken half of it with ferrous sulphate and leave the other half yellow.

4. Let's thicken the yellow dye first. Using your measuring cup, check the amount of dye you have. Per third cup of dye, start with approx. 1/8 tsp gum tragacanth. Pour the dye into your pot and reheat. Then sprinkle in the gum and stir to dissolve and watch the dye thicken.

5. Test the consistency of your paint by painting a test swatch of fabric. If the line bleeds, add a little more gum to thicken further.

6. Pour the paint into a clean glass jar and label clearly. It can be stored in the fridge, but likely won't last as long as the paint that contains ferrous sulphate.

7. Wash out your pot again, then pour in the remaining dye. Add a tiny sprinkle of ferrous sulphate to darken the dye. Watch as it changes colour, and add more if necessary.

8. Now thicken with gum tragacanth, following step 4. Pour the paint into a jar and label.

9. Enjoy using your paint on fabric or paper. Iron fabric after painting and wait a few days before rinsing.

Tip

After dyeing fabric, if you ever have a pot of dye that you've finished with but can't bring yourself to pour away, try simmering (or even boiling) the dye to leave a concentrated ink. This may brown the colour somewhat, but it's a way of making use of every last drop of precious colour! Thicken the concentrated dye to make paint, or keep it as ink.

Rudbeckia (yellow flowers) and purple dahlias

homegrown colour

Have you thought about starting a dye garden but you're wondering where to begin? Flora Arbuthnott shares lots of tips with us. Even if you only have space for a few pots, you can grow some beautiful plants for colour.

Words and photos by Flora Arbuthnott

Hi Flora. It's lovely chatting to you. To get started, can you tell us about your background and your relationship with plants?

I am a natural dyer, grower, and forager concerned with connecting with the land, through practical relationships with the plants and fungi that surround us. I explore wild and cultivated plants to produce a variety of vibrant colours. I observe and learn from the plants that grow around us. I gather wild plants such as meadowsweet, buddleia flowers, oak galls, and dock roots, and grow dye plants in my garden such as madder, woad, and coreopsis.

After studying product design at Glasgow School of Art, I sought to connect with the elements of where our materials come from. I studied permaculture, horticulture, and wild plants. I created my business *Plants & Colour* to bring together my love of nature connection and visual art and design through the craft of plant-based colour.

I have focused on research into the possibilities of plants that are accessible to grow or forage in the UK. I share this work through practical workshops and online courses.

My interest in plants and fungi goes beyond colour. I love to forage for food and make herbal medicines. To be wild is to know how to look after ourselves and to be in an intimate relationship with the plants growing around us, working with the flow of the seasons. There are no weeds – only medicines, foods, dye plants and craft materials. I love to share plant based knowledge, so it can become common knowledge again.

Can you tell us about your beautiful dye garden in Devon?

I have established a dye garden at my house in Devon, and this year, I am also creating a new dye garden next to my studio. I have been sowing the seeds for this garden since the early spring, as well as dividing more established perennial plants from my older garden. I will be planting these out in the run up to midsummer.

Marigold flowers

Orange/red from madder root & yellow from marigold flowers

Growing from seed

I grow annual plants from seed in module trays each year. Coreopsis (*Coreopsis tinctoria*), Marigolds (*Tageres erecta*), hopi black sunflowers (*Helianthus annus*), hollyhocks (*Alcea rosea*), Japanese indigo (*Persicaria tinctoria*) and weld (*Reseda luteola*). I also grow woad (*Istasis tinctoria*) from seed in trays and directly in the ground.

Taking cuttings

If you can get hold of cuttings of perennial plants, this is a cheaper method of propagation for perennial plants that are expensive to buy in large quantities. Perennial plants can also be more difficult to germinate from seed. I like to expand my garden by dividing established plants. This works well with rudbeckia, madder, sage, echinacea, St John's Wort, and dyer's chamomile. I gently dig up side shoots that have viable roots and stem independent of the main plant and pot these up, giving them plenty of water as their new roots establish.

Buying plants

I love going to visit gardens and plant nurseries for inspiration. Sometimes I buy plants that I am curious to try out for their dye. If these plants turn out to be effective, I will then grow more from seed the next year, or take cuttings to expand my supply.

"THERE ARE NO WEEDS – ONLY MEDICINES, FOODS, DYE PLANTS AND CRAFT MATERIALS."

Flora's favourite plants for dyes, inks & paints

Dyer's coreopsis

This is an annual tender flowering plant that I grow from seed each year. The yellow and red flowers give a vibrant orange dye and ink. With the addition of iron, we can make dark green shades.

Dyer's chamomile

Dyer's chamomile is a beautiful evergreen perennial. Once you have this plant established in your garden, you will always have an abundant supply of buttery yellow flowers for the dye pot or ink projects. This plant is high in tannin giving beautiful blacks and greys when combined with iron.

Woad

Woad is our indigenous source of indigo in the UK. Harvest the leaves in the summer to extract the beautiful blue pigment through a fermentation process. I also use the seeds for a blue pigment for painting.

Tagetes marigolds

A rich mustard colour can be created from marigold flowers, as well as yellow and green inks and paints.

Dahlias

Working with dahlias is fascinating because of all of the different colours you can create from the different varieties: greens, oranges, purples, pinks.

Colours from dyer's coreopsis

Dyer's chamomile

Woad

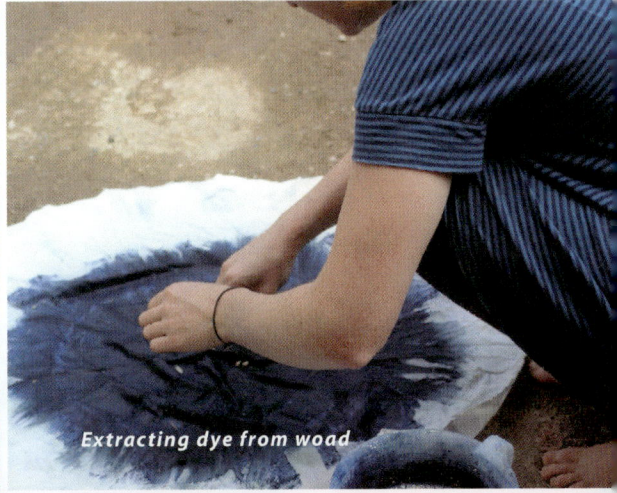

Extracting dye from woad

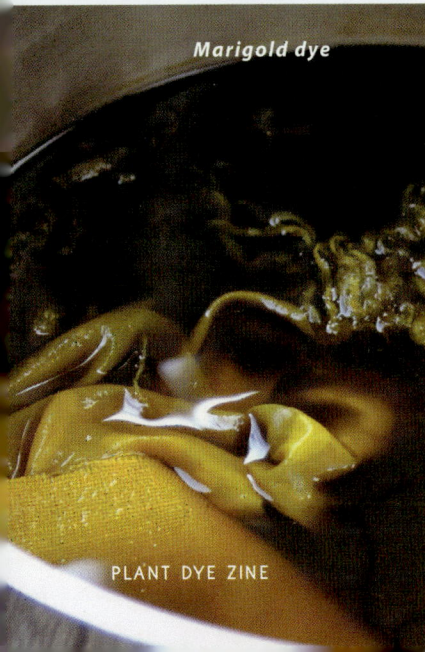

Marigold dye

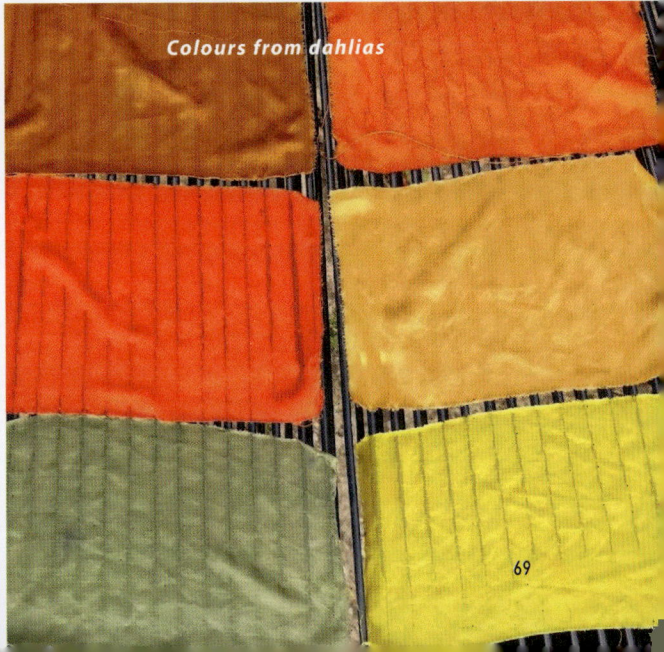

Colours from dahlias

In your garden, is there an overlap between edible and dye plants?

I love how many medicinal herbs offer dye possibilities, such as rosemary, echinacea, sage, bay and willow. Having trained as a vegetable grower before starting to grow dye plants, as well as undergoing training in wild food and herbal medicine, I am interested in how we can have relationships with plants beyond dyeing.

If we have a small space such as a balcony or patio, what do you recommend for growing in pots?

If your space is limited, there are many dye plants you can grow in pots, such as cosmos, tagetes marigold, coreopsis and dahlias.

Personally, I am terrible at growing plants in pots because I always forget to water them! I like to create permaculture gardens where the plants can be resilient without needing many inputs beyond planting and a little weeding.

However, no matter how small a space you have, you can get started right away and begin planting in pots.

How should we begin planning a larger dye garden?

Having moved house a few times over the past few years, I have started five dye gardens. I don't like to do large amounts of digging and it's not good for the soil, so I always start with sheet mulching. This is a method where you cover the ground with cardboard, for between four months and a year. This cardboard blocks the light and kills off the grass and established plants, leaving bare ground that you can plant directly into.

There's a variation to this method where you can begin planting right away. Lay compost on the cardboard and plant directly into this. The cardboard layer will stop a lot of the weeds growing through and they will die over the course of several months. The root systems of the plants will travel down through the cardboard and over time, the layer of cardboard will break down into the soil.

Homegrown dye plants are very special as there is a limited supply until the next season. Does this make you more mindful about what you use in projects?

There are some dye materials such as madder root and weld that are widely available to buy, however there are other special dye plants that are difficult to

Dahlia dye

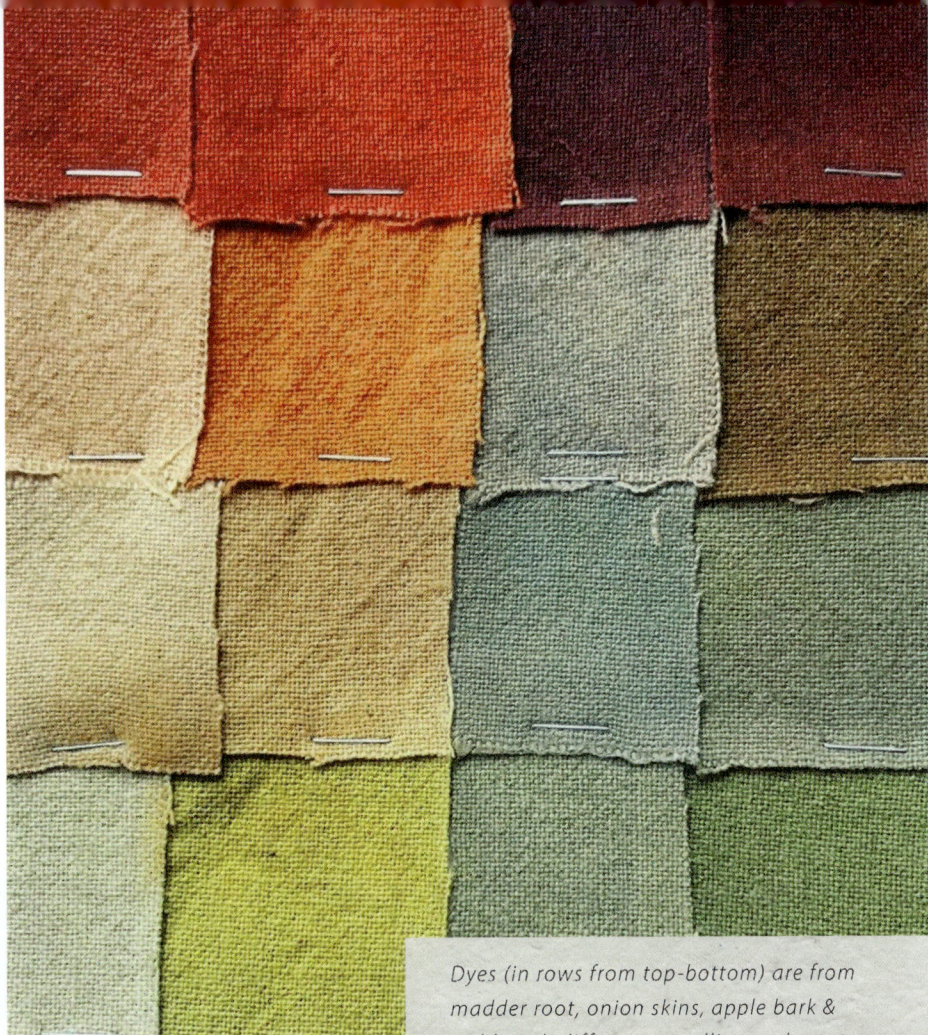

Dyes (in rows from top-bottom) are from madder root, onion skins, apple bark & weld, with different metallic mordants to expand the range of shades.

source, such as hopi black sunflower seeds, coreopsis, and tagetes marigold flowers. All that I grow, harvest and dry each season is all that I have until the next season. This material is precious and I am very conscious of what I use these plants for and make sure that I do not waste a drop of colour. This is why I make dyes, and then use the waste dye bath to make inks, so that every little bit of colour is used and savoured. Some plants such as *Coreopsis tinctoria* are so full of colour that a handful can give a huge quantity of pigment, while dyer's chamomile requires a larger volume to get a deep colour.

Thanks for inspiring us to start a dye garden, Flora! No matter what size space we have, we can all begin now – whether we plant in pots, or have a larger space to play with. Happy planting and dyeing!

Expand the selection of plants in your garden,
balcony or windowsill by growing from cuttings.

growing cuttings

Words and photos by Tina Bettison

There is something deeply nourishing about taking a cutting, watching and waiting to see if it will sprout a root. When you first put that sprig into a jar of water, there is no certainty that it will sprout roots. That first sighting of a tiny root is just joyful. But of course it is only the beginning of the journey.

It's a habit I have inherited from my mother. For as long as I can remember, my mum has begged, borrowed and sometimes stolen sprigs of plants to root and then grow in our garden. Where my dad, a passionate vegetable gardener who fed us from the veggie patch, was excellent at growing from seed, my mum was, and still is, passionate about cuttings.

My dad died aged 90 in 2017. One of my most precious memories is sowing carrot seed with him in the last weeks of his life. My mum, aged 91, and I are creating more precious memories now, taking cuttings to grow and to populate her new garden. After 55 years in our old family home, my mum has moved to a new house in the village with a blank canvas for us to paint with offspring of her beloved plants.

My kitchen and mum's conservatory are full of little bottles and jars, each carefully holding a sprig at various stages of root development, and pots of little plants that are growing up. Mum and I like to leave the cutting in water until it has grown a good tangle of roots, which will give it a better chance of growing well once it's potted up.

While they can be pretty much left to their own devices to grow some roots in water, once you pot them on into compost, they need a little more care and attention. Watering becomes a bit more of an art and some plants need more watering than others. This focus on caring for your cuttings becomes an act of self-care too.

Taking cuttings has another benefit too. Mum has always loved to give and receive cuttings when she visits friends – always on the look out for something different that she doesn't have or offering something new to her visitors. And of course every plant then has a story and a connection to someone.

Even if you have no garden, you can still grow a variety of plants from cuttings and have them in pots. And growing from cuttings costs virtually nothing – just the pot, the compost and some rooting powder if you need it.

A few tips to get you started...

Generally spring and early summer is the best time to take cuttings, but I've taken them later in the year and they have still rooted. It's best to use young or new growth from the parent plant as these will root more easily than old growth. Take the cutting early in the day while it is still full of water. Non-flowering shoots are best. Cut the stem above a bud on the parent plant, taking around 7-10 centimetres so there is plenty of shoot to root.

Herbs like sage, rosemary and mint seem to root well if the stem is left in water until roots appear. I've also used this method for geraniums, pelargoniums, and other hardy or tender perennials. The other method is to dip the stem in hormone rooting powder and then put it directly into damp compost. This method works better for deciduous shrubs such as buddleia, fuchsia and hydrangea.

Whether you use the water or the hormone powder method, you'll need to keep them in a warm and light place but out of hot, direct sunlight.

Don't let your cuttings dry out; they need to be quite moist for the first few weeks until roots are established. A plastic bag over the top of the pot can help to keep the environment moist; you will need to remove the bag at least twice weekly for 15 minutes or so for ventilation. You don't need to use a bag if the cutting is in water.

Leaves may die or rot off, in which case remove them. The plant will most likely be rejuvenating itself, so persevere; sometimes it looks like it's not doing anything and then suddenly you'll notice a new shoot or a little growth spurt. Not every cutting will root. It can be a little trial and error too, but it's fun learning what works and what doesn't.

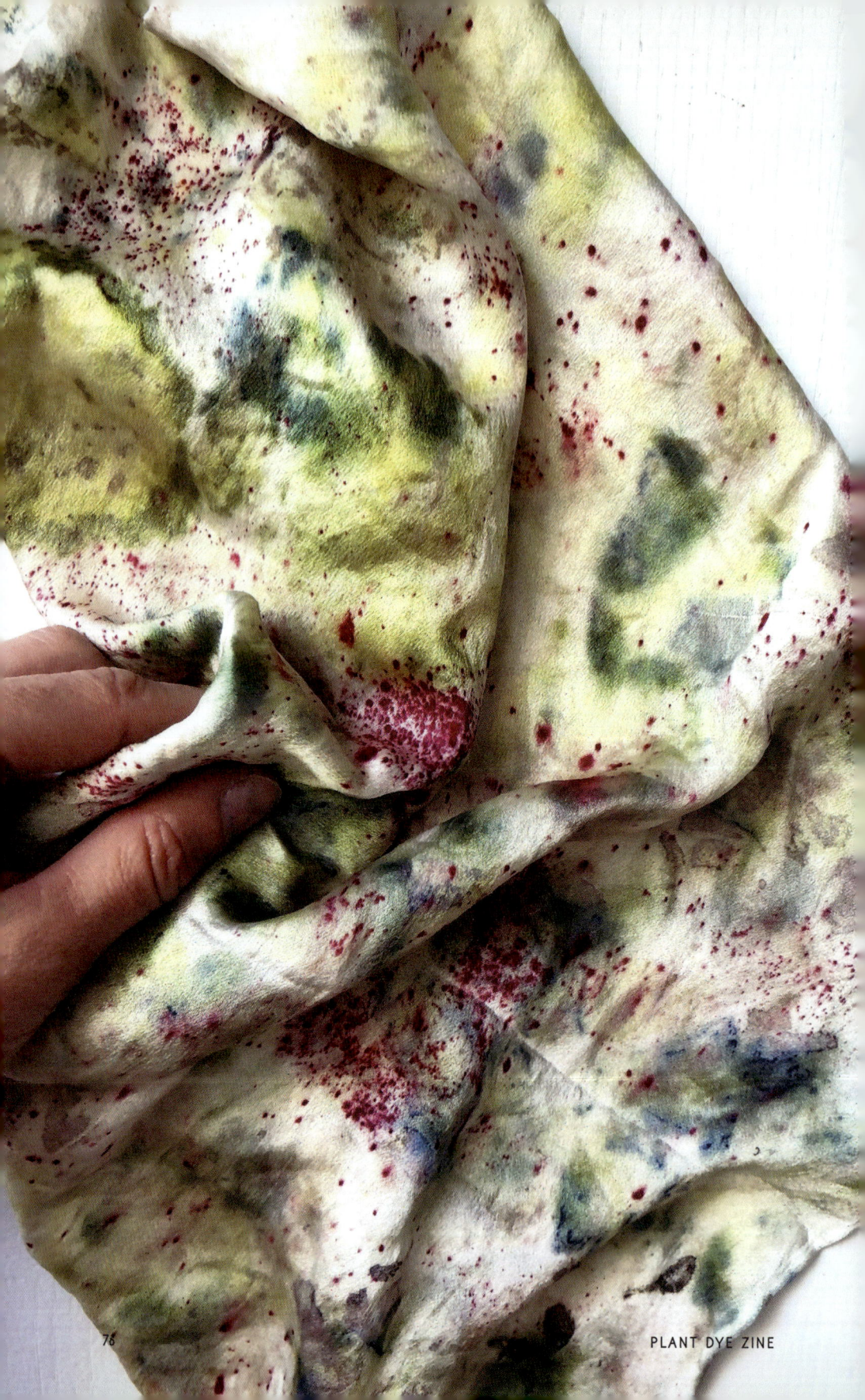

bundle dyeing with flowers

Words and photos by Maggie Pate

Growing flowers can be a bittersweet practice. The months of labour and then the treat of a fragrant bloom, only to then watch it wilt. What joy to give florals a second life by capturing their hues on fabric – to record a season, a moment in time, a celebration, a feeling.

Recently I did just this with the flowers I received for my birthday. Once their petals had begun to curl and dry, I gathered the flowers with the boldest and brightest colours to bundle dye with them. The silk scarf ended up looking like one of Monet's Water Lilies.

What you need

- Flowers

- Any other natural dye extracts or powders that you wish to use

- Fabric – I used silk, but cotton and linen work well too

- Synthrapol or soda ash

- Aluminium potassium sulphate (for silk) or aluminium acetate (for cellulose fibres)

- Water

- Stainless steel pot

- Lid that fits over pot securely

- Tongs and/or wooden spoon

- Mesh strainer

- Undyed string (coloured string will transfer its colour to the fabric)

- Scissors

- Rubber gloves

Safety notes

- Before you begin, please read the safety guidelines on page 105.

- If you're doing this activity with children, do the scouring and mordanting steps without them.

- Wear a face mask if you use aluminium acetate to avoid inhaling the fine powder.

- Wear gloves to protect your hands and wrists from the steaming pot of water.

Let's make our bundle

1. Scour your scarf with ½ teaspoon of synthrapol in a stainless steel pot filled halfway with water. As a less toxic alternative to synthrapol, you can use soda ash (15g soda ash per 100g fabric). First, add the soda ash to a jar of luke warm water and mix well, then pour this mixture into your large pot of water. Set the stove top burner to medium heat to create a simmer and every so often rotate the fabric with a wooden spoon to release the air bubbles. This process should take 60 minutes. Then give the scarf a rinse in the sink. Discard the liquid from the pot.

2. Start your mordant bath. These quantities are for a 30 x 30 inch scarf. To dye a larger quantity of fabric, increase the amount of alum.

   For silk add 2 tablespoons of aluminium potassium sulphate and fill halfway with water.

   For cellulose fibres add 2 teaspoons of aluminium acetate to your pot of water.

   With the stove top burner on medium heat, simmer your scarf for 80 minutes rotating every 15 minutes with a wooden spoon to release the air bubbles. Then do a rinse bath in the sink with cool water.

3. Collect together your blooms. Use bright and bold coloured flowers. For this silk I used eucalyptus leaves, red roses, red geraniums, dark purple tulips, as well as yellow, orange, pink and purple ranunculus.

4. Gather any other dye materials that you'll be sprinkling onto the fabric such as food waste or powdered dye extracts.

5. Place the wet fabric on top of a clean flat surface. Stretch the fabric until there are little to no wrinkles or folds.

6. Measure to find the centre of your scarf, since you will be laying out your design on half of the fabric.

7. Lay the dye materials onto the fabric making sure they are as flat as possible. You may have to take the flowers apart and arrange the petals. Mind the centre line to make sure there isn't a white stripe going through the middle of your fabric.

8. Once you're happy with the arrangement, fold the blank half of fabric over the half with the plants.

9. Liberally cut a piece of string to use to tie up the bundle.

10. Roll your halved fabric up into a cylinder. I like to call this *sushi rolling* or *making a fibre burrito*. Then wrap and lace the string around the long sausage and tie it up.

Steaming the bundle

11. Fill your pot with water and place the mesh strainer inside it. Make sure the water does not fill into the strainer.

12. Turn your stove onto medium heat, then place the lid on the pot to let the steam begin to accumulate.

13. Once the condensation begins to gather on the inside of the lid, add your bundle inside the mesh strainer. You may need to coil it depending on how large it is.

14. Steam your bundle for about an hour. Wearing gloves, check on it every so often. Use the tongs to rotate and flip it, and also check the water level and add more if needed.

15. After an hour, let the bundle cool before handling it, then cut the string and unroll it.

16. Rinse off the flowers with cool water, then hang to dry away from direct sunlight.

Portrait by Linda Campos: lindarcampos.com

How long will the prints last?

Some flower dyes will last longer than others. To preserve the colours, store the scarf in a dark place when it's not being worn, and wash with cool water and a natural laundry detergent. For the longest lasting results, use plants that are known to have the best levels of colourfastness. If your scarf fades, simply redye it with the next bouquet of flowers that you have.

make + decorate a flower press

Make your own flower press, then pound violas and pansies into the plywood as decoration.

Words and photos by Rebecca Desnos

I've been playing around with flower hammering for a few years, since learning from Samorn Sanixay. Each time I hammer onto fabric, I fall in love with the way that the wooden board receives the prints through the layers of fabric. My board has built up multiple layers of botanical prints and it feels like a piece of living artwork that evolves over time.

For this project, I decided to deliberately hammer straight onto wood and make a flower press. You could also make a lovely wooden wall hanging.

Choosing plants

Hammering onto wood is a bit different to cloth, as wood doesn't absorb dye as quickly as fabric. If your plants are very juicy, they can easily splatter across the wood and create a mess. It's a balance between finding leaves and flowers that transfer their colour to the wood, but aren't too moist. Equally, if a leaf is waxy, then it won't transfer its colour to wood very easily.

Pansies and violas work beautifully on wood. The petals are highly pigmented but not too juicy. Lilac, deep purple and dark red varieties work best as these colours will last the longest. Yellow and orange flowers fade quickly. This method will no doubt work with countless other flowers and leaves. I've had success with young, tender rose leaves – both green and red leaves.

To check for pigment, rub a flower or leaf onto a piece of fabric or paper and see if it stains. Of course, use your common sense and only try plants that are not toxic. Wherever you live in your world, you will have a unique selection of plants to try.

Before creating any artwork, I suggest you find a piece of scrap wood and do some tests. Sometimes it's best to lay a leaf face down, and other times face up gives a clearer print.

Making your press

I'm basing the following design on a homemade flower press that I inherited as a young child. You may choose to use only two pieces of plywood in your press. I had the wood cut to size by a timber merchant, so it was just a question of drilling the holes.

Gather your materials and tools:

- 2 or 3 pieces of plywood 20 x 20 cm, at least 8 mm thick.

- Sandpaper to smooth edges of plywood.

- 4 long bolts (6 mm diameter) with accompanying wing nuts and washers. Try to get the longest bolts possible. The longer, the better as it gives you more space for plants within the press.

- Electric drill and drill bit at least 1 size larger than bolts.

- Work bench and clamps.

- Ruler and pencil.

- Craft knife.

- Several pieces of cardboard for inside the press. Cut into 20 x 20 cm squares then cut off the corners.

To pound the plants, you also need:

- A hammer or mallet.

- Piece of fabric e.g. cotton sheeting.

Let's begin

1. Measure the position to drill the holes. I marked the centre of the holes in the corners, 2 cm from each edge.

2. Measure the thickness of your bolts and find a drill bit that is at least 1 size larger than this. You want the holes to be slightly bigger so the bolts thread through easily.

3. Arrange your pieces of wood in a stack* then clamp onto your work bench. Drill the 4 holes. Try your best to ensure the drill goes through straight and even, and not crooked, otherwise your flower press will be difficult to assemble. * Placing an extra piece of scrap wood at the bottom of your stack can give a cleaner drill hole and stop the plywood splintering.

4. Cut your pieces of cardboard to use inside the press.

Preparing the flowers

1. Allow any insects to crawl away.

2. Trim off the stems and also carefully snip the fleshy bulbous part off the back of the flowers (pictured below). Don't trim too far down as the flower will fall apart. For larger pansies, it can be helpful to trim away some of green sepals (the "leafy" parts on the back). The less moisture behind the petals, the better. This will allow the petal prints to come through clearer.

3. Decide on the pattern that you'd like to create and lay the flowers face down. You will get a second flower print on the piece of fabric that is laid on top.

Hammering

1. Lay your piece of wood (with flowers laid out) onto a hard, stable surface such as concrete. Add a protective covering to your surface, as required. We need to hammer onto a firm surface without any bounce. For this reason, hammering with the wood laid on carpet doesn't work.

2. Lay your piece of fabric on top and begin to hammer the flowers through the fabric. Hammer in a firm and controlled way and watch as the prints begin to reveal themselves on the fabric. It's helpful to hammer the outer edge of a petal first and work towards the centre.

3. Keep hammering until all of the flowers are done, checking as you go to make sure that all parts of the flower have come through to the fabric layer.

4. Peel off the fabric to reveal the print. Be careful not to smudge the flowers at this stage.

5. The flowers are likely to be stuck to the wood, not the fabric, so let them dry fully before peeling off flowers. If you remove them when wet, the print won't be as clear.

6. You get a bonus print on fabric, so allow this to also dry fully before peeling off any petals.

Finishing your press

1. When the flowers stuck to the wood are dry, begin to carefully peel them off. Some parts may peel off intact like a piece of tissue paper, but other parts may need to be scratched off. I like to use a small piece of card to gently rub off the petals. As long as the flowers are dry, then the print shouldn't be affected by light rubbing.

2. Decide if you will leave the wood unfinished, or apply oil as a sealant. Linseed oil is a good choice.

How long will the flower prints last?

The degree of colourfastness varies according to the plants you use. Yellow flowers fade the quickest, which is why I like to stick to darker pigments such as purple violas and pansies. Red and pink geranium petals also hold their colour well, as do red and orange marigolds. Many leaf prints last well. Often leaf prints will gradually shift from green to more of a khaki-tan colour.

Whether or not you put your prints in the sunlight will also affect the longevity of the colours. Flower presses are stored out of the light, so your design should last well. However, if you'd like to create some artwork for the wall, then it's a good idea to test some prints on scrap wood and monitor the fading.

If the flower prints on your press eventually fade, you could hammer a new design on top. The ghosting from the fading prints can be beautiful.

Photos on pages 94 - 97 by Autumn Layne Photography: autumnlaynephoto.com

PLANT DYE ZINE

flower pressing

Words by Tricia Paoluccio

We chat with Tricia Paoluccio from *Modern Pressed Flower* about how she got started pressing flowers, how to pick flowers responsibly, and Tricia takes us through her process step by step!

When did you begin flower pressing?

I've been pressing flowers for as long as I can remember. I grew up on a 40 acre almond farm in Central California. My parents are not farmers in the traditional sense. My mom keeps tearing out the trees to build wildlife habitats. She recently decided to pull out a few more acres to grow a wildflower meadow. It's not the most practical choice, but it's beautiful, and she likes to make the wildlife and the commuters happy.

My mom not only instilled a deep respect for nature, but also a love of beauty and handmade things. She never allowed us to buy a card in a store — we always had to make our own. So my card making has been a lifelong practice! My brother and dad, who are both inventors, made me the flower presses which I still use to this day.

Is flower pressing something that you've always done alongside acting?

I moved to New York City to pursue my goal of becoming an actor, and sold my cards and collages on the street and to little boutique stores. I remember my sweet aunt commissioning me every holiday to make handmade cards to help me out! My rent was only $500 a month, so I could cobble together a living selling my art and doing odd jobs, while I auditioned for shows.

Even after I got my first Broadway show when I was 25, I never stopped making things. I always had little projects happening on my dressing room tables. It's such a zen activity, very instinctive and calming. I've been very fortunate to have made a living as an actor since then, and I joke to my friends that I need my acting career to pay for my art habit. Collage-making and working with pressed botanicals is something I always return to.

Do you like to capture special memories by pressing flowers from particular places or occasions?

The first time I added pressed flowers to a wedding invitation was for my own wedding in 1999. I pressed little cherry blossoms that looked like delicate rose

buds and glued them onto handmade white paper with a deckled edge. So simple and beautiful. I would choose the exact same design today! I wish I had kept one, but I never even put together a wedding album, and this was long before smart phones or social media. I wish I could say that I've kept flowers to capture special memories, but I'm not really a journal keeper. I do love handmade Valentine's and Mother's Day cards adorned with pressed flowers and like to encourage mailing paper cards over emails. I think it's a lovely tradition.

Where do you gather your flowers?

I get the vast majority of my flowers from California — from my parent's, my sister in law's and our neighbour's beautiful gardens. Everyone is so generous to share their bounty. My family also owns a little cabin with hundreds of acres in the CA foothills in a town called Moccasin. This land is undeveloped, and there are hundreds of wildflowers and weeds that I love to press: lupines, baby blue eyes, Indian paintbrush, and butterfly mariposa lily to name a few. My brother also has a cabin in Lake Tahoe, and I get my mountain wildflowers from his backyard there: woods' rose, buttercups, leafy aster….too many to list!

When picking flowers, what should we keep in mind in terms of collecting responsibly and with respect for nature?

The vast majority is gathered from our own property or the property of friends. As a Californian, I was schooled to never pick a wildflower in the wild, especially our California state poppy. I picked a few poppies from our own yard before the

field was mowed down: even that felt scandalous! You never want to deprive others of seeing nature's beauty. Never pick the first or the last of anything, and don't be wasteful. Never pick more than you intend to use. I measure that by only picking what I can carry in one hand!

Do you have any tips for storing pressed flowers?

I store all my botanicals in my flower presses. These presses can be made by hand with two pieces of wood, cardboard rounds and recycled paper. I separate the flowers (usually by thickness), layer them with paper and cardboard, and stack them on top of each other to keep them secure so they don't shift.

Your colours are so vibrant! Can you share any tips for keeping colours bright?

Always pick your botanicals on a dry day so that there is no moisture on the flower. Sandwich the botanicals in between many layers of paper and cardboard. The paper absorbs water from the flower, so don't skimp on the layers. The colours remain the most vibrant if the pressing process is done patiently. They don't like moisture or light.

What kind of adhesive is best for collages?

I use rubber cement when I make cards. It's a very forgiving glue when you are using mixed media, and I like to be able to rub off the excess adhesive so that the flower and papers blend seamlessly. For my larger pieces, I use pH-neutral or acid free glue. It dries clear and doesn't turn yellow.

Do you have a favourite flower?

My favourite flowers are the wildflowers found in the foothills, particularly Lily of the Nile which boasts a large purple spray of blossoms that presses beautifully and keeps its vibrant colour. Another favourite is Indian's paintbrush which comes in all shades of coral and red. They look stunning amongst the rocky terrain of the foothills. I feel like the luckiest treasure hunter in the world to be able to go to California as often as I do and to have access to such beautiful abundance in nature.

"GATHER FLOWERS ON A DRY DAY. ANY DROPLET OF WATER ON A PETAL WILL TURN THAT FLOWER BROWN."

Flower pressing guide

It takes me ten times the amount of time to gather and press flowers than it does to make anything with them! Patience is your friend when it comes to pressing flowers. Do not rush the process.

1. Gather your flowers in the afternoon on a dry day. Do not pick in the morning when there might be dew, or after rain, or after you have watered your garden. Any droplet of water on a petal will turn that flower brown.

2. Pick flowers in all stages of growth — from bud, to half way bloomed, to fully open. I like to press plants including tendrils from bushes and tiny leaves and weeds with roots. I find all of nature so interesting and even the tiniest humble weed can become a beautiful pressing.

3. Only pick what you can carry in one hand. If you try to press too much, they could wilt before you even get the chance to press them all!

4. Place the first piece of cardboard in the press and then put at least 5 pieces of paper on top.

5. Layer the same type of flower on that piece of paper without letting them touch, and don't crowd. You want the flowers to be the same thickness, which is why I press the same type of flower on each layer.

6. Put at least 5 pieces of paper on top of that and then a cardboard round.

Photos on pages 98 - 101 by Marilyn Days: marilyndays.com

7.   Repeat until you reach the top. Screw the wing nuts down gently – do not squeeze.

8.   Every few hours check your press and you will see you need to gently screw down more as the layers have loosened.

9.   The next day, undo your press, being careful not to disturb the pieces of paper that sandwich the flowers. Replace the cardboard rounds and paper from your stock and re-layer everything into your press with dry paper and cardboard. You don't want to let your flowers sit in a damp press for many days.

10. After about two weeks, your flowers should be ready to use for collage or card making!

Making a press

To make a press like mine, cut two pieces of thick oak wood measuring 10" square. Use bolts that are 6 - 8" long and gather four wingnuts. I use cardboard cake rounds and recycled paper to sandwich in between — at least 10 pieces of paper (cut square) in between the cardboard.

Pressing a rose

This is one method that you can try. Using a sharp knife, carefully slice the rose in half, to remove some of the bulk. Then place the flower in your press and add several layers of paper on top to absorb the moisture from the flower. Then follow the flower pressing steps on the previous page for the best results.

appendix

- Pretreating fabric in soya milk

- Safety guidelines

- Bibliography

- Other publications by Rebecca Desnos

- Keeping in touch

Pretreating fabric in soya milk

Soya (soy) milk can be used as a pretreatment on fabric, acting as a binding agent between plant fibres and plant dyes. The soy protein binds to cellulose fibres, making them more receptive to plant dyes. This improves colourfastness and helps achieve darker dye colours.

The following recipe pretreats up to 400g of fabric. Buy soya milk that contains as few additives as possible. The recipe below uses store bought milk; homemade soya milk is more concentrated so will need to be diluted further. The aim is to coat the fibres with several layers of diluted milk – a thick layer will lead to uneven dyeing results later on.

Try to do this on a cool day so the milk stays as fresh as possible. Discard the milk if it goes off. This is a summary of the method in *Botanical Colour at your Fingertips* (2016).

Method

1. Pour 1 litre of soya milk into a bucket and add 5 litres of water. Add your clean fabric in there and mix well. If the fabric isn't fully submerged, add more water. Leave to soak for 12 hours.

2. Remove fabric, then squeeze out milk. Spin out the excess liquid in the washing machine (spin cycle with no water). Hang to dry.

3. Dip the fabric in the bucket of milk again to receive an even coating, squeeze by hand, then spin out the excess in the washing machine. Allow to dry.

4. Do a final dip in the milk, squeeze out, then spin out in the washing machine. Use a quick wash cycle to clean your empty machine.

5. Leave the fabric to dry then set aside for a week before painting or dyeing so the soy protein can cure on the fabric.

Fabric soaking in buckets of soya milk, outside on a cool day.

Safety guidelines

These are some common sense guidelines to always keep in mind:

- Take care when identifying plants and if you need help, consult a reliable book or a knowledgeable friend. Remember that some plants are toxic, so only dye with plants that you can correctly identify. Be extra cautious when children are helping.

- Use a separate set of equipment reserved for dyeing – not your kitchen pots, sieve, wooden spoons etc.

- When you are heating dye pots, make sure you have good air flow. Keep a window open and don't stand over a steaming pot and breathe in the vapour.

- Wear gloves to protect your skin from dyes.

- Wear thick gloves when opening steaming pots, as the steam can scald your wrists quickly.

- Wear a mask when working with fine powders such as aluminium acetate.

- Keep dyes away from children, pets and food.

- Carefully label any jars of dye that you store in the fridge so that everyone knows it's not edible! Do the same for dye that you freeze.

Background photo by Annie Spratt / photo on page 104 by Rebecca Desnos

Bibliography

CAUTHEN, JOYCE H. 2013. *Out of Whole Cloth: The Life of Bettye Kimbrell*. Published by Joyce Cauthen.

DEAN, Jenny. 2010. *Wild Colour: How to grow, prepare and use natural dyes*. Mitchell Beazley.

DESNOS, Rebecca. 2016. *Botanical Colour at your Fingertips*. Published by Rebecca Desnos.

LOGAN, Jason. 2018. *Make Ink: A Forager's Guide to Natural Inkmaking*. Abrams.

PATE, Maggie. 2018. *The Natural Colors Cookbook*. Page Street Publishing.

Photo by Annie Spratt

Other publications by Rebecca Desnos

rebeccadesnos.com

Botanical Colour at your Fingertips is a gentle introduction to dyeing fabric and yarn with plants. It focuses on dyeing cellulose fibres with soya (soy) milk as a binder.

There is colour potential everywhere! Find out how to unlock colour from plants that you already have at your fingertips.

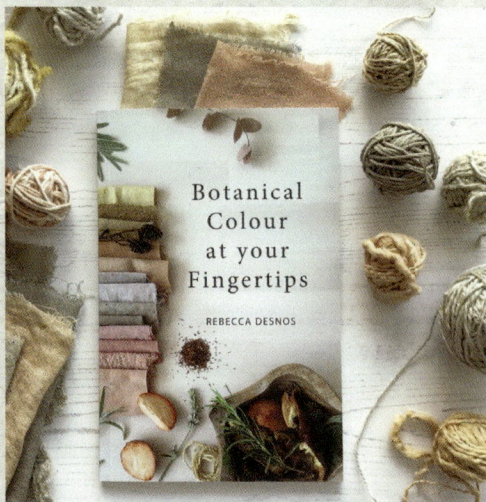

Learn how to dye wood with homemade plant dyes.

I've been dyeing beads for years and for the first time, I've shared my dyeing process so you can dye your own. This eBook isn't limited to beads; I share tips for painting other wooden surfaces too – even small items of furniture! The possibilities with plant dyes are endless!

Thanks for joining us

Let's keep in touch!

Join my mailing list
for musings on plants, creativity & simplicity.
www.rebeccadesnos.com/newsletter

Follow me on Instagram
@rebeccadesnos

Send an email
info@rebeccadesnos.com

Portrait by Siobhan Watts / Background photo by Kai Pilger

Printed in Great Britain
by Amazon